THREE CAPE COD

BOTANICAL WALKS

IN DENNIS, MA

Gary R. Sanford, Ph.D.

ISBN: 9798618089791

CONTENTS

ACKNOWLEDGMENTS

I am grateful for manuscript review by Jason S. Sanford. His suggestions have greatly improved this booklet.

INTRODUCTION

This booklet provides checklists of common and conspicuous plants growing along three trail systems located in, and maintained by, the town of Dennis, MA. Details on plant ecology, topography, soils, and wetlands are also included. Trails are within the Princess Beach, Indian Lands, and Flax Pond conservation areas, which are free to the public. They traverse a variety of landscape features that include nearly level to steep slopes, swales, depressions, abandoned cranberry bogs, ponds, streams, freshwater wetlands, and salt marshes. Walking is easy, and chances are that not more than one or two people will find their way past you during an outing.

The checklists offer a challenge to spot the presence of each species, as well as an aid in species identification. Beyond this, relationships between plants, plant communities, and landscape features can be explored. Plants occur in spatial patterns for a multitude of reasons, including the species reproductive strategy, phenotypic plasticity (changes in morphology or physiology in response to environmental conditions), physiological tolerance ranges, competitive ability, and the recurrence of similar environments within a landscape. For example, sweet pepperbush (*Clethra alnifolia L.*) grows in clumps because of its ability to reproduce by root suckering. The dense thickets of this shrub offer a competitive advantage that excludes many plants, and its ability to live in waterlogged soils results in a recurring pattern of occurrence in wetlands across the landscape.

Environmental conditions to keep in mind include severity of slope and the direction it is facing, position on slope, presence of depressions or swales, distance from water bodies, distance from salt water, potential to receive salt water spray, depth to groundwater, flooding or signs of past flooding, and soil characteristics. Plant growth is affected by localized weather conditions. Examples include: distance to the ocean which can affect growing season, location on slope which can affect the number of frost free days, and exposure which can affect plant desiccation from wind or ice.

Plant habit is important. Size and height affect availability of light. Shoot density affects competitive ability as well as successful reproductive strategies. Root morphology affects access to water and nutrients. Natural root grafting can enhance access to water and nutrients, and potentially result in the transfer of organic compounds between plants.

Another important consideration is the occurrence of past perturbations. Historically, most of the Cape was logged and placed in agriculture. Most agriculture has since been abandoned, and our forests are still recovering. Fire has played an important role in our landscape, as well as disease and insect infestations.

One of the most important and generally the easiest environmental condition to spot is the presence of wetlands. Different species have different affinities for wetlands. The checklists include species wetland status in the northeast. They are classified as one of the following: obligate, facultative wetland, facultative, facultative upland, and upland. Appendix 1 provides definitions for these groupings.

Each trail description includes discussions of topography, soils, and wetlands. Portions of USGS quadrangles provide information on hills and depressions. Orthophotographs (aerial photographs that have been adjusted so that scale is uniform across the image) show characteristics of vegetation, and the location of wetlands. After each checklist, a brief ecological examination of one or two species is provided.

Down-loading trail maps from the town website is encouraged.

It is a good idea to know how to identify poison ivy when walking on any trail on Cape Cod. Protection against ticks is also recommended.

Gary R. Sanford

PLANT IDENTIFICATION

If you are not able to identify many of the common plant species growing on the Cape, it is suggested that an identification manual be brought along on your walk, and utilized as seen fit. The following approach can help ID a specimen by restricting your focus to just a few species, thus narrowing down your search. In addition, it will sharpen your observation skills relative to ecological conditions.

Identify Your Relative Environmental Position

Look at the surrounding topography. Are you on top of a large hill, on a slope, near the bottom of a slope, or in a flat area or depression with signs of flooding? Is the terrain dominated by hills and depressions? If so, are you in the depression or on the hill? What direction does the slope face?

Water availability is one predominant characteristic that determines local plant distributions. The least amount of water will be located on top of a hill or its slope. Groundwater flow generally follows topographic gradients (there are localized exceptions), and groundwater level will be found closer to the surface near the toe of a slope. Often it will reach near the surface in low flat areas and depressions. Side slope springy areas are also a possibility, but given Cape soil conditions, are not often found here. South and west facing slopes are generally drier than north and east facing slopes. Swales and depressions accumulate more water than adjacent slopes. Observations on the relative water availability, in conjunction with the wetland status (see Appendix 1) of listed species, can suggest possible candidates in the identification process.

Wetland or Upland?

Decide if the plant is located in a wetland or upland. Flooded areas are obviously going to be wetlands, however areas which are only temporarily flooded, or simply have groundwater near the surface for periods of time, are common wetland types. These wetlands will often have a dense thick shrub layer that reaches a height of 6 feet (2 m) or more. Upland shrubs are often only a few feet high, and occupy sites higher on a slope than wetlands. There are many exceptions to these plant height generalizations. Typically, wetlands will have a lush appearance compared to nearby uplands.

Determine Growth Habit

Growth habit simply refers to the life form of a plant. The USDA system (see Appendix 2) is used in trail checklists (Tables 1, 2 & 3). Within checklists, species are grouped by their growth habit, and, within each grouping, arranged by their wetland status. Plants growing in uplands include "upland" and "facultative upland" species. Those found in wetlands include "facultative wetland" and "obligate" species. "Facultative" species are often found in both upland and wetland conditions.

Once determinations concerning location (upland versus wetland), and growth habit are reached, select a representative specimen for identification. Evaluate species listed in the chosen grouping to determine the specimen's identity. Keep in mind two things. The tables are not intended to be complete floristic lists, but simply represent common and conspicuous plants observed on the trails. Your plant may not be on the list. Also, the vast majority of species can be found both in uplands or wetlands. Evaluate other candidates based upon their wetland indicator status.

As a hypothetical example, consider the top of a hill that is dominated by trees. Shrub growth is limited to plants only a few feet high. Clearly, this is an upland. Select a specimen tree for identification, and then examine the trail list for species catalogued as upland or facultative upland trees. In this example, six species are listed, and some of these can be eliminated immediately because your specimen is an evergreen pine. This leaves only two species to choose from. Use your manual to choose between the two species (or read further).

Gary R. Sanford

UPLAND OAKS AND PINES

Across the Cape, you will see oaks and pines as dominant trees, so here are some characteristics helpful in identifying a few of these species.

Pitch pine (*Pinus rigida*) can easily be identified from its needle clusters (fascicles), each of which contain three needles that can reach 5 inches (13 cm) in length. Mature tree bark consists of thick flat plates and deep furrows, and sprouts of needles may often be seen growing on the trunk. Female cones are from 2 to 4 inches (5 to 10 cm) long; a short, stout prickle develops on each cone scale.

White pine (*Pinus strobus*) is often conspicuous by its large size, commonly over 100 feet (30 m) tall, and can even reach 150 feet (46 m) in height. Mature trees are branch-free on the lower boles, and the thick bark has scaly long ridges with furrows. The five needle fascicles that are up to 5 inches (13 cm) long make it easy to identify. Both male and female cones appear on the same tree, and the female cones grow to between 4 and 7 inches (10 and 18 cm) in length.

Oak trees fall into two categories here on the Cape, red and white. Both groups have variable shaped leaves with sinuses (indentations between lobes) ranging from deep to shallow. Sometimes the full range of leaf shapes exist on the same tree; shallow sinuses can occur in shade while deep sinuses develop in full sun. The tips of leaf lobes are smooth in the white oak group, while species in the red oak group have bristle-tipped lobes.

Within the white oak group, **white oak** (*Quercus alba*) is very common on the Cape.   This slow growing species can reach heights of 60 to 80 feet (18 to 24 m). The plant has 4 to 7 inch (10 to 18 cm) long leaves with smooth lobe tips, and the bark is distinctive. Bark has a grayish light color, and is scaly on small stems but irregularly platy or blocky on larger trunks.

Within the red oak group of trees, black oak, red oak, and scarlet oak should be mentioned. They are harder to identify than the smooth-leafed white oak, and, since they hybridize, often have intermediate forms. Try to use more than one characteristic.

Black oak (*Quercus velutina*) is a medium-sized, deciduous tree that will usually grow to about 60 to 80 feet (18 to 24 m). The leaves, with 5 to 9 bristle-tipped lobes, can vary from 4 to 10 inches (10 to 25 cm) in length. Glossy leafs have undersides covered in pubescence (downy hairs) that is shed in late summer; buds are entirely covered with a light colored pubescence, and acorn cups have loose scales that stick out near the top of the cup. The nearly black bark of mature trees is thick with deep vertical furrows, and has horizontal breaks.

Northern red oak (*Quercus rubra*) is a medium to large tree, and will usually grow to about 65 to 100 feet (20-30 m) in height. Leaves can range from 4 ¾ to 8 inches (12 to 20 cm) in length, and have 7 to 11 bristle-tipped lobes. Sinuses reach less than half the distance from lobe tips to the midrib. Look for smooth reddish petioles (leaf stalks). Underside of leaf ranges from gray to light yellowish-green in color with short tufts of wooly hair in the axils of veins.   Acorn cups are shallow, and have reddish-brown pubescent (hairy) scales with dark margins. The pointed ovoid buds have chestnut-brown pubescent scales. Mature tree bark is dark gray to black with shallow vertical furrows separating light colored scaly ridges. Ridges usually reach within 1 to 2 feet (.3 to . 6 m) of the ground.

Scarlet oak (*Quercus coccinea*) is a relatively short-lived, but fast growing, deciduous tree that usually grows 60 to 80 feet (18-24 m) tall. It frequently has downward arching branches and an enlarged trunk base.   Leaves can range from 2 ¾ to 6 ¼ inches (7 to 16 cm) in length and have 5 to 9 bristle-tipped lobes. Sinuses nearly reach the midrib (more than half-way from lobe end), and lobes are distally expanded. Leaves are shiny light green above, and have tufts of hair in the axils of veins underneath. Acorn cups are glossy dark reddish-brown, and cover ⅓ to ½ of the nut. Terminal buds clustered at ends of branches are reddish-brown with pubescence near apices.   Tree bark has shallow vertical furrows separating light colored scaly ridges. Ridges usually stop 6 to 12 feet (2 to 4 m) above the ground.

Gary R. Sanford

PRINCESS BEACH
CONSERVATION AREA

Kinnikinnick (*Arctostaphylos uva-ursi*) along northern trail.

The Princess Beach Conservation Area (see Figure 1) is located about 3.3 miles (5.2 km) north of Route 6 and 0.6 miles (1 km) south of Cape Cod Bay. Its western border lies adjacent to Scargo Lake; the eastern portion of the preserved region is part of the Paddock Farm Conservation Area. Access to Princess Beach is from Scargo Hill Road.

The hill, seen as a density of contour lines in the lower left of Figure 1, is a kame that reaches an elevation of 160 feet, (49 m), and was formed when outwash deposits filled a hole in the glacier during the last glacial period. The landform was left when ice melted away. Conservation areas lie northeast of the hill on an outwash plain. Generally, elevations drop by about 20 feet (8.8 m) in a northeasterly direction from trail heads to the Paddock Farm area. Strongly sloping areas are limited.

The Natural Resources Conservation Service has mapped 6 soil map units within the area, with well drained soils present over most of the land. Textures range from loamy fine sand to coarse gravelly sand with boulders. Except for wetlands, depth to groundwater is 6 ft (2 m) or more. The sandy soils limit water holding capacity so that vegetation must frequently contend with droughty conditions, and, as a result, seedling mortality may be exacerbated.

Wetlands are located on the Paddock Farm area as shown in Figure 2. The soil is classified as Berryland Mucky Loamy Course Sand, which is found in very poorly drained flat areas with a water-table at or near the surface during fall, winter, and spring. The Department of Environmental Protection has mapped both shrub swamp and wooded swamp here, and wooded canopies have varying ratios of deciduous and evergreen trees present.

Upland (non-wetland) vegetation consists of a deciduous tree dominated zone in the southern third of the property, and a mixed deciduous evergreen wood over the remainder (see Figure 2). The trail system runs primarily through the mixed deciduous evergreen woods dominated by pitch pine and black oak. Trees fall largely within the 5 to 10 inch (13 to 25 cm) diameter range, and thus provide an impression of a moderately young wooded area. The sapling layer is not well-developed; shrubs are occasional and patchy with black huckleberry most common. Ground cover is also limited with patches of lowbush blueberry present. One striking feature along the northern trail consists of large patches of foliose lichens. Woody debris is sparse; snags with cavities are occasionally present. Generally, much of the area presents a park-like appearance. However, near the bottom of the slope, and in depressions on the slope, thickets of horsebrier flourish suggesting more water is available for plant growth. Another facultative plant, eastern poison ivy, is abundant at the bottom of the slope along the disturbed roadsides.

Wooded wetlands were observed during walk over. This wetland type is located in the Paddock Farm Conservation Area where a trail leads down to its edge (see Figure 2). During the dry season, it is possible to continue across the wetland to the opposite side. In contrast to the pine/oak woods, the wetland presents a lush thick green aspect. Red maple, with occasional pitch pine, form the tree canopy, and a thicket of sweet pepperbush dominates the shrub layer. Cinnamon fern can be found in the ground cover. Table 1 lists common or conspicuous plant species observed along the trails.

Figure 1. Portion of USGS quadrangle showing Princess Beach Conservation Area. Contour interval = 10 ft. Quadrangle from Bureau of Geographic Information, Commonwealth of Massachusetts, Executive Office of Technology and Security Services. Trails from Town of Dennis Trail Map.

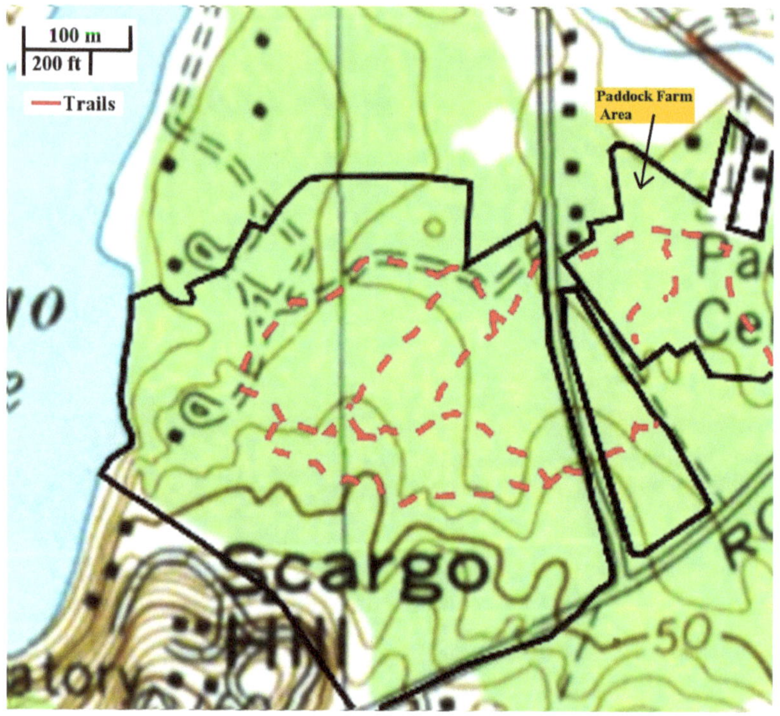

Figure 2A. Orthophotograph of Princess Beach ConservationArea from Bureau of Geographic Information, Commonwealth of Massachusetts, Executive Office of Technology and Security Services. Trails from Town of Dennis Trail Map.

Figure 2B. Orthophotograph of Princess Beach Conservation Area. DEP wetland boundary from Bureau of Geographic Information, Commonwealth of Massachusetts, Executive Office of Technology and Security Services. Trails from Town of Dennis Trail Map.

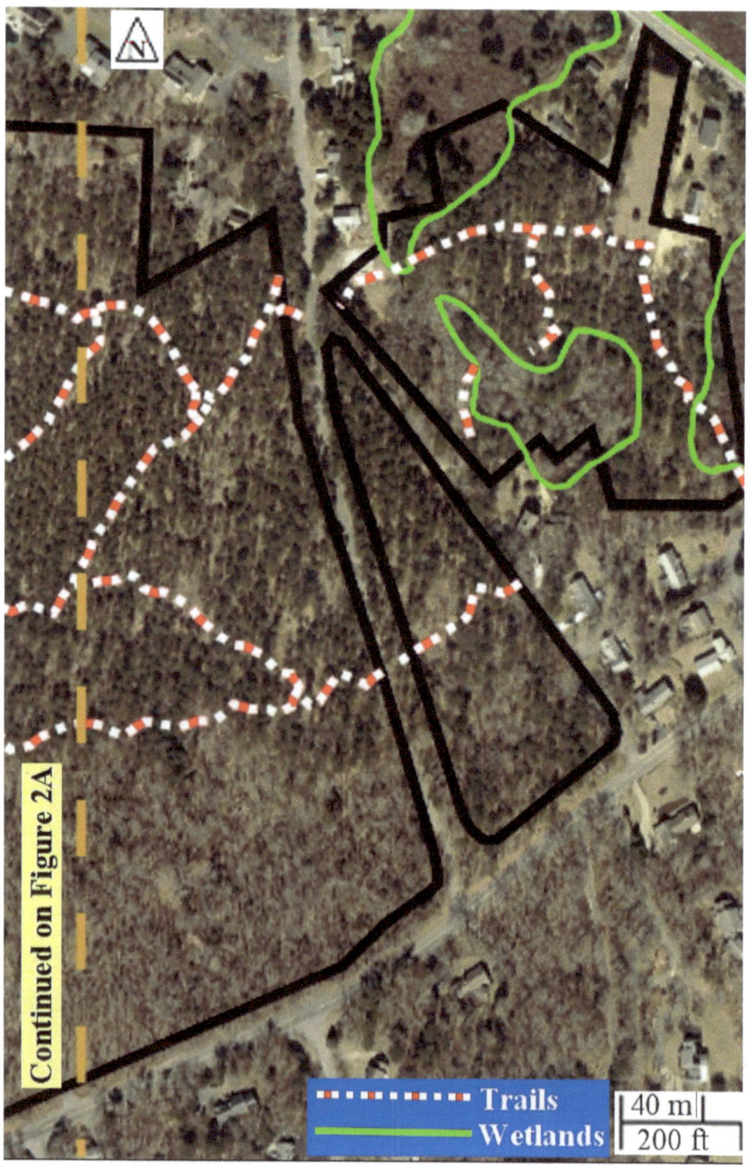

Table 1. Checklist of species noted along Princess Beach Conservation Area trails.

✓	Scientific Name	Common Name	Wetland Status[1]	Growth Habit[2]
	Quercus coccinea Münchh.	scarlet oak	upland[3]	Tree
	Quercus velutina Lam.	black oak	upland[3]	Tree
	Pinus rigida Mill.	pitch pine	FACU	Tree
	Pinus strobus L.	eastern white pine	FACU	Tree
	Quercus alba L.	white oak	FACU	Tree
	Quercus rubra L.	northern red oak	FACU	Tree
	Robinia pseudoacacia L.	black locust	FACU	Tree
	Acer rubrum L.	red maple	FAC	Tree
	Nyssa sylvatica Marsh.	tupelo	FAC	Tree
	Quercus ilicifolia Wangenh.	bear oak	upland[3]	Shrub/Tree
	Ilex opaca Alton	American holly	FACU	Shrub/Tree
	Prunus serotina Ehrh.	black cherry	FACU	Shrub/Tree
	Sassafras albidum (Nutt.) Nees.	sassafras	FACU	Shrub/Tree
	Morella pensylvanica (Mirbel) Kartesz	northern bayberry	FAC	Shrub/Tree
	Clethra alnifolia L.	sweet pepperbush	FAC	Shrub
	Gaylussacia baccata (Wangenh.) K. Koch	black huckleberry	FAC	Shrub
	Smilax rotundifolia L.	horsebrier	FAC	Shrub Vine
	Vaccinium corymbosum L.	highbush blueberry	FACW	Shrub

✓	Scientific Name	Common Name	Wetland Status[1]	Growth Habit[2]
	Arctostaphylos uva-ursi (L.) Spreng.	kinnikinnick, bearberry	UPL	Shrub/Subshrub
	Chimaphila umbellata (L.) W.P.C. Barton	pipsissewa	upland[3]	Subshrub
	Comptonia peregrina (L.) Coult.	sweet fern	upland[3]	Shrub/Subshrub
	Gaultheria procumbens L.	wintergreen, eastern teaberry	FACU	Shrub/Subshrub
	Vaccinium angustifolium Aiton	lowbush blueberry	FACU	Shrub/Subshrub
	Toxicodendron radicans (L.) Kuntze	eastern poison ivy	FAC	Forb/herb/Shrub/Subshrub/Vine
	Aralia nudicaulis L.	wild sarsaparilla	FACU	Forb/herb/Subshrub
	Osmunda cinnamomea L.	cinnamon fern	FACW	Forb/herb
	Carex pensylvanica Lam	Pennsylvania sedge	upland[3]	Graminoid
	Deschampsia flexuosa (L.) Trin.	wavy hair-grass	FACU	Graminoid
	Celastrus orbiculatus Thunb.	oriental bittersweet	UPL	Vine
	Parthenocissus quinquefolia (L.) Planch.	Virginia creeper	FACU	Vine

[1]See Appendix 1 [2]See Appendix 2. [3]Not listed on the National Wetland Plant List.

Additional Ecological Information: Pitch Pine

Pitch pine (*Pinus rigida*) can easily be identified from its needle clusters (fascicles), each of which contain three needles that can reach 5 inches (13 cm) in length. Trees can reach heights of 82 feet (25 meters) or more and 3 feet (1 meter) in diameter. Individual plants can reach 200 years in age.

Except for a few outlying populations, general distribution along the eastern U.S. is from central Maine to northern Georgia, and is most common on the Atlantic coastal plain. It is common and extensive on the Cape, occurring as a dominant species in upland (non-wetland) woods, and can also be found in wooded wetlands, particularly those which are on the drier side.

A number of characteristics make the species particularly well adapted for life on the Cape. Recognized as a member of early seral stages, it can quickly become established after significant fires, and, during secondary succession, after fields and pastures are abandoned. This ability is promoted by seed germination favoring exposed mineral soils. Although seeds have relatively large wings, they are not dispersed far by wind. Wildlife may play a significant role in seed dispersal. Seeds can remain viable for a year after dispersal.

During spring, male cones release pollen which is wind transported to female cones. Cones mature over the course of the following two years, and at maturity open and release seeds immediately. Other cones can remain closed until heated by fire (serotinous cones) before releasing seeds. The proportion of serotinous to nonserotinous cones increases in fire prone areas. Seed predation by birds and squirrels can be high.

Once germinated, seedlings develop a tap root that can grow longer than the shoot for the first few years. Mature trees have tap roots that can extend down over ten feet, and lateral roots that reach out over thirty feet. The exploitation of such a large soil volume provides an advantage to plants in the nutrient-poor sandy soils with low water holding capacity common on the Cape. Lateral roots occur within a few inches of the soil surface, and the tap root can penetrate the water table; characteristics that are beneficial in a wetland. Root grafts occur between trees which presumably allows sharing of water, nutrients and sugars. Nutrient uptake may be increased because of mycorrhizal associations which are common in pitch pine. The rooting system also provides stability during high winds and reduces windthrows.

Pitch pine often has drooping branches along the lower trunk. Persistent dead branches are high in resin. These characteristics increase fuel availability, and hence risk of fire damage. Trees are protected by thick bark that insulates the delicate cambium tissue, and dormant buds located within the base of the tree. After injury or top kill from fire (or other reasons such as insect damage), basal buds may break dormancy and develop a new shoot system. Reforestation is improved when fire opens serotinous cones to release seed onto exposed mineral soils.

Pitch pine is considered shade intolerant, and except in very harsh conditions, will be replaced by hardwoods. In the case of the Princess Beach Conservation Area, oaks can be expected to replace the pines.

INDIAN LANDS
CONSERVATION AREA

Indian Lands salt marsh system.

The Indian Lands Conservation Area (see Figure 3) is located 2.7 miles (4.35 km) north of Nantucket Sound near Route 6. Its western border forms the bank of Bass River. The Cape Cod Rail Trail and a power line lie along the northern border. Despite its distance from the ocean, the shoreline and much of the marshland within the area is flooded by high salinity estuarine water. Parking is available at the Cape Cod Rail Trail parking lot on Main Street just before crossing the rail trail from the south. Access to the conservation area is along the power line corridor.

Interior marsh systems divide the upland area into two portions; each portion has its own trail network (see Figures 3 and 4). The south-western trail drops roughly 15 or 20 feet (4.6 or 6.1 m) to the marsh; it travels through woods, across a narrow isthmus, and onto a hilly island that borders the river on one side, and a marsh on the other. The north-eastern trail system allows access to a peninsula of hilly upland. This trail first drops about 5 feet (1.5 m) to a rickety bridge over a small perennial stream. Both of the trail systems encircle uplands adjacent to the river, and each of these uplands rise about 15 feet (4.6 m) to their high points.

Outwash deposits form land features on the site, and upland (non-wetland) soils are classified by the Natural Resources Conservation Service as Carver Coarse Sand, which is subcategorized based upon slopes that range from 0 to 35%. More than 80% of the uplands have either gently sloping (3-8%) or strongly sloping (8-15%) relief. The Carver units are composed of deep coarse-textured soils that are excessively well drained, and have very rapid permeabilities both in the subsoil and substratum. Soil water holding capacities are low, and depth to seasonal high groundwater tables exceed 6 feet (2 m). Similar to soils in the Princess Beach uplands, Carver soils tend to be droughty.

The Department of Environmental Protection has mapped vegetated wetlands on the site (see Figure 4). Wooded swamp and shallow marsh are present in Figure 4A. They occur on Freetown Coarse Sand which has been used in the production of cranberries, and therefore has an upper layer of sand (used in cranberry production). It is a very deep, level, and very poorly drained soil. Below the sand, to a depth of 65 inches (165 cm) or more, occurs muck and mucky peat. The mineral surface layer has very rapid permeability, while underlying organic material has moderate to moderately rapid permeability. Water holding capacity is very high; seasonal high water table is within 1.5 feet (.5 m).

Salt marsh is present in Figures 4B and 4C. Salt marsh soils are classified as within the Ipswich - Pawcatuck - Matunuck Complex These three soils may be present individually, or in combination with one another in the mapping unit. They are inundated by tides twice a day. Ipswich soil has 65 inches (165 cm) or more of peat, Pawcatuck has about 22 inches (56 cm), and Matunuck has about 13 inches (33 cm).

Uplands (non-wetlands) are dominated by deciduous and evergreen trees (see Figure 4). Along trails, common or dominant trees include scarlet and white oaks, and both pitch and white pines. Saplings are limited, and undergrowth is often sparse. Common shrubs include black huckleberry and bear oak.

Trails lead down to Bass river, and generally follow along either salt marsh or open water. Wetland species become more common at these lower elevations, even though they may be growing in uplands. Northern bayberry and horsebrier are examples. Herbaceous ground cover, such as wild sarsaparilla, is able to get a foot hold within canopy breaks.

Common freshwater wetland species include red maple trees, and highbush blueberry and sweet pepperbush shrubs. While freshwater wetlands are limited on site, the salt marsh system is spectacular. Marsh elder grows at the upper levels of the salt marsh; saltmeadow cordgrass and smooth cordgrass form the marsh matrix. Common reed (*Phragmites australis*) can be seen in patches along the marsh edge. *P. australis* is an invasive species with a wide range in salinity tolerance. It is common along and into the upper boundaries of salt marshes, as well as in freshwater wetlands. Table 2 lists common or conspicuous plant species observed along the trails.

Figure 3. Portion of USGS quadrangle showing Indian Lands Conservation Area. Contour interval = 10 ft. Quadrangle from Bureau of Geographic Information, Commonwealth of Massachusetts, Executive Office of Technology and Security Services. Trails from Town of Dennis Trail Map.

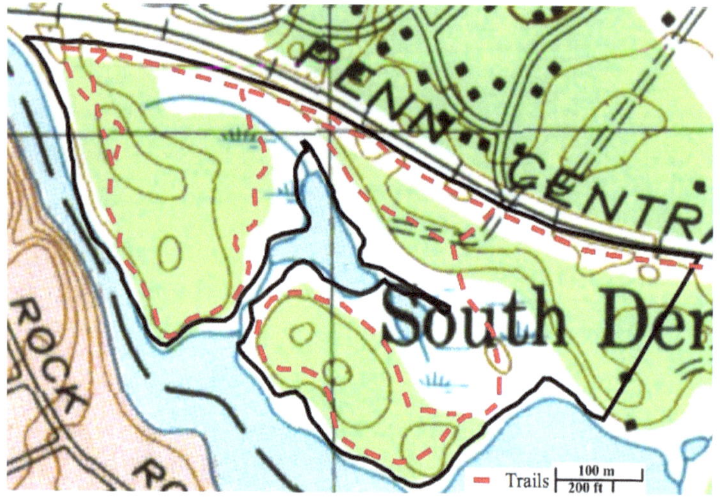

Figure 4A. Orthophotograph of Princess Beach Conservation Area. DEP wetland boundary from Bureau of Geographic Information, Commonwealth of Massachusetts, Executive Office of Technology and Security Services. Trails from Town of Dennis Trail Map.

Figure 4B. Orthophotograph of Princess Beach Conservation Area. DEP wetland boundary from Bureau of Geographic Information, Commonwealth of Massachusetts, Executive Office of Technology and Security Services. Trails from Town of Dennis Trail Map.

Figure 4C. Orthophotograph of Princess Beach Conservation Area. DEP wetland boundary from Bureau of Geographic Information, Commonwealth of Massachusetts, Executive Office of Technology and Security Services. Trails from Town of Dennis Trail Map.

Table 2. Checklist of species noted along Indian Land Conservation Area trails.

✓	Scientific Name	Common Name	Wetland Status[1]	Growth Habit[2]
	Quercus coccinea Münchh.	scarlet oak	upland[3]	Tree
	Quercus velutina Lam.	black oak	upland[3]	Tree
	Juniperus virginiana L.	eastern red cedar	FACU	Tree
	Pinus rigida Mill.	pitch pine	FACU	Tree
	Quercus alba L.	white oak	FACU	Tree
	Quercus rubra L.	northern red oak	FACU	Tree
	Acer rubrum L.	red maple	FAC	Tree
	Nyssa sylvatica Marsh.	tupelo	FAC	Tree
	Quercus ilicifolia Wangenh.	bear oak	upland[3]	Shrub/Tree
	Prunus serotina Ehrh.	black cherry	FACU	Shrub/Tree
	Morella pensylvanica (Mirbel) Kartesz	northern bayberry	FAC	Shrub/Tree
	Viburnum dentatum L.	southern arrowwood	FAC	Shrub/Tree
	Gaylussacia baccata (Wangenh.) K. Koch	black huckleberry	FACU	Shrub
	Clethra alnifolia L.	sweet pepperbush	FAC	Shrub
	Smilax rotundifolia L.	horsebrier	FAC	Shrub/Vine
	Vaccinium corymbosum L.	highbush blueberry	FACW	Shrub
	Gaultheria procumbens L.	wintergreen, eastern teaberry	FACU	Shrub/Sub-shrub

✓	Scientific Name	Common Name	Wetland Status[1]	Growth Habit[2]
	Vaccinium angustifolium Aiton	lowbush blueberry	FACU	Shrub/Sub-shrub
	Toxicodendron radicans (L.) Kuntze	eastern poison ivy	FAC	Forb/herb/ Shrub/Sub-shrub/Vine
	Iva frutescens L.	marsh elder/ Jesuit's bark	FACW	Forb/herb/ Subshrub
	Aralia nudicaulis L.	wild sarsaparilla	FACU	Forb/herb/ Subshrub
	Carex pensylvanica Lam	Pennsylvania sedge	upland[3]	Graminoid
	Phragmites australis (Cav.) Trin. ex Steud,	common reed	FACW	Graminoid/ Shrub/ Subshrub
	Spartina alterniflora Loisel.	smooth cordgrass	OBL	Graminoid
	Spartina patens (Aiton) Muhl.	saltmeadow cordgrass	OBL	Graminoid
	Celastrus orbiculatus Thunb.	oriental bittersweet	UPL	Vine
	Parthenocissus quinquefolia (L.) Planch.	Virginia creeper	FACU	Vine

[1]See Appendix 1 [2]See Appendix 2. [3]Not listed on the National Wetland Plant List.

Additional Ecological Information: smooth cordgrass and saltmeadow cordgrass

Both **smooth cordgrass** *(S. alterniflora)* and **saltmeadow cordgrass** *(S. patens)* are common along the Atlantic and Gulf coasts from Newfoundland to Texas. They form the matrices of our familiar salt marshes in New England. These salt marshes are commonly divided into two zones in New England, where smooth cordgrass dominates the low marsh habitat below mean high tide, and saltmeadow cordgrass is prevalent in the lower elevations of the high marsh. Smooth cordgrass will also be seen along banks of ditches and streams where the species is immersed in saline water for long durations.

Smooth cordgrass generally ranges in height from 2 to 6 feet (0.61 to 2 m) depending upon site conditions, while saltmeadow cordgrass ranges from 1 to 4 or 5 feet (0.3 to 1.2 or 1.5 m). Smooth cordgrass has 0.1 to 1 inch (3 to 25 mm) wide flat leaf blades that typically are 12 to 20 inches (30.5 to 50.8 cm) long, and taper to an inward-rolled tip. Saltmeadow cordgrass has 0.1 to 0.2 inch (3 to 7.6 mm) wide rolled leaf blades that typically are 6 to 12 inches (15 to 30.5 cm) long. Saltmeadow cordgrass has scabrous (rough) leaf margins, while leaf margins on S. alternaflora are smooth, although there may be a few scattered teeth.

Spartina alterniflora

Smooth cordgrass is capable of surviving in fluctuating water depths, and is tolerant of sea water salinities. It can dominate areas with salinities ranging from 3 to 5 percent, and an average water depth of 4 inches (10.2 cm). The species is restricted to the lower marsh by competition from saltmeadow cordgrass, but, in the absence of the latter, can readily grow in the upper marsh habitat. It has a competitive advantage over saltmeadow cordgrass in the low marsh environment because of its ability to oxygenate its roots and rhizosphere in oxygen deprived soils.

S. alterniflora reproduces both sexually and vegetatively, but successful seedling establishment is mostly restricted to bare areas in the marsh. Because the species occurs in dense stands, seedling establishment is inhibited at these locations, and vegetative reproduction is of prime importance. Smooth cordgrass develops an extensive rhizome system from which new tillers develop.

Spartina patens

Saltmeadow cordgrass grows in saline to brackish marshes, and even into beach and foredune environments. Its ability to live in saturated soil is enhanced by aerenchyma tissue (spongy tissue with air spaces) that forms in its roots under flooded conditions. This ability allows it to maintain its presence just above smooth cordgrass stands, but other high marsh species, such as black grass (Juncus gerardii) and saltgrass (Distichlis spicata) competitively exclude saltmeadow cordgrass from the upper reaches of the high marsh.

S. patens can reproduce both vegetatively and sexually. It can grow in peat deposits of varying depths, and also in various types of mineral soils. Its rolled up leaves and thick cuticle help it tolerate salt spray.

Gary R. Sanford

FLAX POND
CONSERVATION AREA

Trail along Flax Pond.

The Flax Pond Conservation Area (see Figure 5) lies north of Route 6, and is 2.2 miles (3.5 km) south of Cape Cod Bay. Access is from Setucket Road in Dennis. Flax pond is a kettle hole formed from a block of glacial ice that was surrounded by sediments. Upon melting, a depression was left that filled with water. Natural wetlands and abandoned cranberry bogs occupy the rest of the site's lowlands.

The Natural Resources Conservation Service has mapped four soils in the uplands: Carver coarse sand, Plymouth loamy coarse sand, Eastchop loamy fine sand, and Deerfield loamy fine sand. Roughly three quarters of the site has these soils with Carver coarse sand being most common (about 70% of the upland areas). The Carver units are composed of deep coarse-textured soils that are excessively well drained, and have very rapid permeabilities both in the subsoil and substratum. Soil water holding capacities are low, and depth to seasonal high groundwater tables exceed 6 feet (2 m). The Plymouth and Eastchop soils make up most of the remaining uplands; like Carver soil, they exhibit rapid permeabilities, low water holding capacities, and depths to seasonal high groundwater tables exceeding 6 feet (2 m). All three soils tend to be droughty. The Deerfield soil occurs in depressions, swales, and low areas adjacent to streams and ponds. Water holding capacity is low, but depth to seasonal high water is only 1.5 to 3 feet in winter and early spring. Portions of this soil could occur in drier parts of wetlands along their edges.

Site elevations range from about 25 feet (7.6 m) to 90 feet (27.4 m). Roughly half the uplands have soils that are classified as nearly level to gently sloping (0 to 8%); the remaining uplands are classified as ranging from strongly sloping to steep (8 to 35%). Wetlands occupy low flat areas.

The Department of Environmental Protection (DEP) has mapped vegetated wetlands on the site (see Figure 6). Shrub swamp, deciduous wooded swamp, mixed trees (deciduous and evergreen) wooded swamp, and shallow marsh are present. The abandoned cranberry bog (see Figure 5 for location) currently supports all four wetland types and they occur on Freetown Coarse Sand. This soil has been used in the production of cranberries, and therefore has an upper layer of sand (used in cranberry production). It is a very deep, level, and very poorly drained soil. Below the sand, to a depth of 65 inches (165 cm) or more, occurs muck and mucky peat. The mineral surface layer has very rapid permeability, while underlying organic material has moderate to moderately rapid permeability. Water holding capacity is very high; seasonal high water table is within 1.5 feet (.5 m).

A small shrub swamp adjacent to the northern shore of Flax pond has been mapped as Freetown and Swansea mucks. Freetown soil has muck and peat to a depth of 65 inches (165 cm) or more; Swansea soil has muck to a depth of about 3 feet (.9 m). Muck is highly decomposed organic matter; peat is largely undecomposed organic matter. These soils are similar in having moderate or moderately rapid permeabilities in the organic layers, very high water holding capacity, and seasonal high water tables at or near the surface for most of the year.

As one walks towards Flax pond from the parking area, a wetland can be seen to the west of the trail. DEP has divided this swamp into a southern portion of mixed deciduous and evergreen canopy cover, a central portion of shrub swamp in the power line corridor, and a northern portion of deciduous canopy cover.

Flax pond is roughly circular, and has a wooded shoreline within the conservation area. An exposed red maple root system supporting a shoreline tree can be seen on reaching the pond. This is a good reminder of an important aspect of plant ecology. A major portion of the plant body occurs out of sight underground, but its morphology and physiology are key to survival ability in various environments.

Although this pamphlet tends to classify the environment into either wetlands or uplands, it should be emphasized that there is a continuum of conditions across an area. Inkberry is a facultative wetland plant that can also grow in non-wetland areas. Its presence in swales may be indicative of wetter conditions (but not necessarily a wetland) compared to adjacent locations, since the swale would accumulate water from up-gradient sources.

Uplands (non-wetlands) are dominated by varying ratios of deciduous and evergreen trees (see Figure 6). Along trails, common or dominant trees include white oak, black oak, scarlet oak, and pitch pine. A thick ground cover is often present that includes black huckleberry, lowbush blueberry, and wintergreen. Table 3 lists plant species observed along the trails.

Figure 5. Portion of USGS quadrangle showing Flax Pond Conservation Area. Contour interval = 10 ft. Quadrangle from Bureau of Geographic Information, Commonwealth of Massachusetts, Executive Office of Technology and Security Services. Trails from Town of Dennis Trail Map.

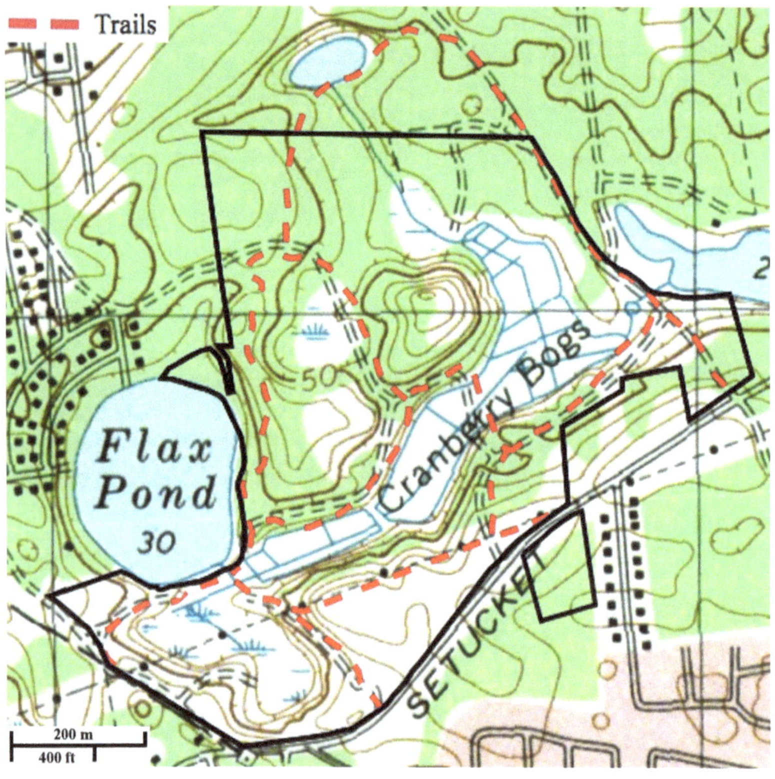

Figure 6A. Orthophotograph of Flax Pond Conservation Area. DEP wetland boundary from Bureau of Geographic Information, Commonwealth of Massachusetts, Executive Office of Technology and Security Services. Trails from Town of Dennis Trail Map.

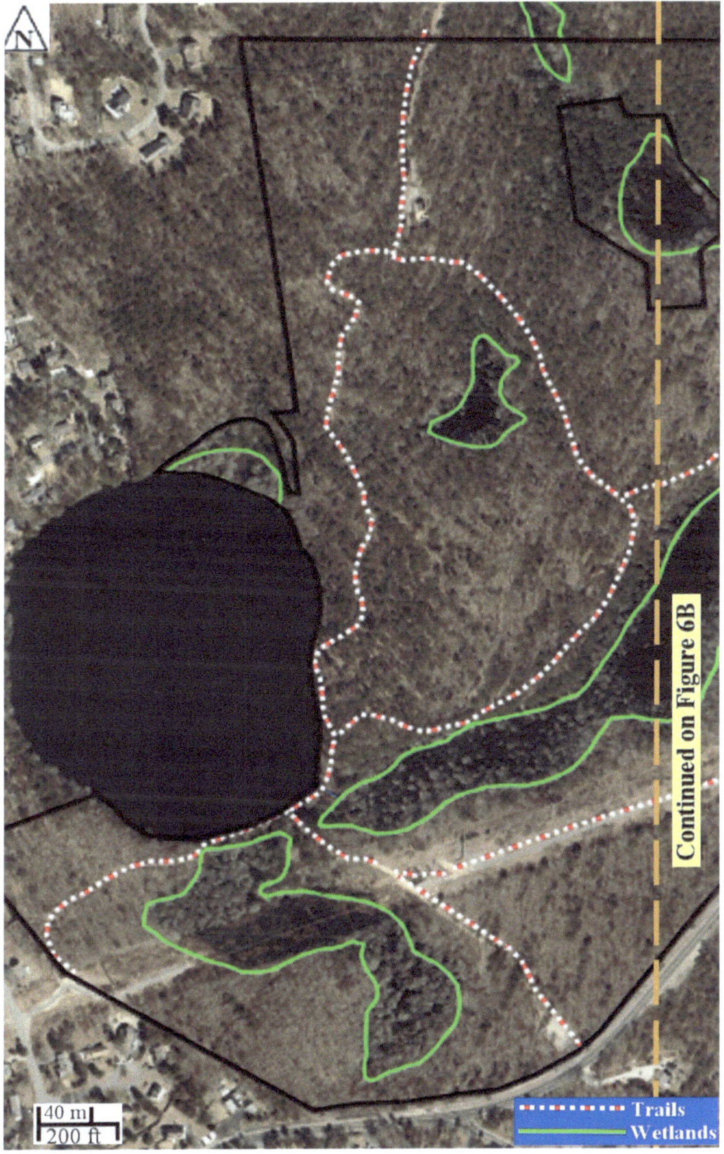

Figure 6B. Orthophotograph of Flax Pond Conservation Area. DEP wetland boundary from Bureau of Geographic Information, Commonwealth of Massachusetts, Executive Office of Technology and Security Services. Trails from Town of Dennis Trail Map.

Table 3. Checklist of species noted along Flax Pond Conservation Area trails.

✓	Scientific Name	Common Name	Wetland Status[1]	Growth Habit[2]
	Quercus coccinea Münchh.	scarlet oak	upland[3]	Tree
	Quercus velutina Lam.	black oak	upland[3]	Tree
	Pinus rigida Mill.	pitch pine	FACU	Tree
	Quercus alba L.	White oak	FACU	Tree
	Quercus rubra L.	northern red oak	FACU	Tree
	Acer rubrum L.	red maple	FAC	Tree
	Nyssa sylvatica Marsh.	tupelo	FAC	Tree
	Prunus serotina Ehrh.	black cherry	FACU	Shrub/Tree
	Sassafras albidum (Nutt.) Nees.	sassafras	FACU	Shrub/Tree
	Morella pensylvanica (Mirbel) Kartesz	northern bayberry	FAC	Shrub/Tree
	Cytisus scoparius (L.) Link	Scotch broom	upland[3]	Shrub
	Rhus copallinum L.	winged sumac	UPL	Shrub/Tree
	Gaylussacia baccata (Wangenh.) K. Koch	black huckleberry	FACU	Shrub
	Ligustrum vulgare L.	European privet	FACU	Shrub
	Lonicera morrowii A. Gray	Morrow's honeysuckle	FACU	Shrub
	Clethra alnifolia L.	sweet pepper bush	FAC	Shrub

✓	Scientific Name	Common Name	Wetland Status[1]	Growth Habit[2]
	Kalmia angustifolia L.	sheep laurel	FAC	Shrub
	Smilax rotundifolia L.	horsebrier	FAC	Shrub/Vine
	Ilex glabra (L.) Gray	inkberry	FACW	Shrub
	Vaccinium corymbosum L.	highbush blueberry	FACW	Shrub
	Chimaphila umbellata (L.) W.P.C. Barton	pipsissewa	upland[3]	Subshrub
	Gaultheria procumbens L.	wintergreen, eastern teaberry	FACU	Shrub/ Subshrub
	Pteridium aquilinum (L.) Kuhn	brackenfern	FACU	Subshrub
	Vaccinium angustifolium Aiton	lowbush blueberry	FACU	Shrub Subshrub
	Toxicodendron radicans (L.) Kuntze	eastern poison ivy	FAC	Forb/herb/ Shrub/Sub-shrub/Vine
	Aralia nudicaulis L.	wild sarsaparilla	FACU	Forb/herb/ Subshrub
	Maianthemum canadense Desf.	Canada mayflower	FACU	Forb/herb
	Phytolacca americana L.	American pokeweed	FACU	Forb/herb
	Solidago sp.	goldenrod		Forb/herb
	Thelypteris palustris Schott	eastern marsh fern	FACW	Forb/herb
	Carex pensylvanica Lam	Pennsylvania sedge	upland[3]	Graminoid

✓	Scientific Name	Common Name	Wetland Status[1]	Growth Habit[2]
	Parthenocissus quinquefolia (L.) Planch.	Virginia creeper	FACU	Vine
	Vitis labrusca L.	fox grape	FACU	Vine

[1]See Appendix 1 [2]See Appendix 2. [3]Not listed on the National Wetland Plant List.

Additional Ecological Information: Red Maple

Red maple (*Acer rubrum L.*) grows 30 to 90 feet tall with a trunk diameter of up to 4 feet, but often is seen with multiple trunks stemming from previous logging. Two leaves occur opposite each other along twigs; leaves have 3 (sometimes 5) lobes. Look for "V" shaped sinuses (leaf notches) to differentiate red maple from sugar (Acer saccharum) and Norway (Acer platanoides) maples that have "U" shaped sinuses. Silver maple (Acer saccharinum) leaves have "V" shaped sinuses, but the leaves are larger and usually have 5 long lobes.

Red maple is a widely distributed tree in eastern North America, partly because of its wide environmental tolerance ranges. It is able to do well in both wetlands and uplands. It survives in both sunny and moderately shady circumstances, in high or low nutrient soils, and in a wide range of soil types, textures, and pH. Red maple often forms almost pure stands in many forested wetlands. Mortality results from prolonged flooding year after year, hence a dead red maple swamp may be indicative of an increased flood regime within that wetland. Nevertheless, the tree can survive on hummocks in wetlands with prolonged flooding.

Root habit varies with soil conditions which allows it to grow in a wide variety of moisture regimes. Seedlings produce short tap roots with long laterals on wet sites, and long taproots (straight vertical primary root) with shorter laterals on dry sites.

Flowering occurs before leaf-out, and prolific seed production is common. The winged seeds mature, disperse, and germinate in early summer when one can often find hundreds of tiny seedlings, but most will perish over the course of a few years. Up to 95 percent of viable seeds germinate within the first 10 days following dispersal, while a few seeds can overwinter in the duff and germinate the following growing season.

APPENDIX 1

The "wetland status" used in Tables 1, 2, and 3 are obtained from ratings listed in the "2016 National Wetland Plant List". Short indicator rating definitions, shown below, are taken from Lichvar, R. et al., July 2012. Lichvar et al. also provide longer definitions which identify wetland features and provide plant examples.

OBL (Obligate Wetland Plants)—Almost always occur in wetlands.

FACW (Facultative Wetland Plants)—Usually occur in wetlands, but may occur in non-wetlands.

FAC (Facultative Wetland Plants)—Occur in wetlands and non-wetlands.

FACU (Facultative Upland Plants)—Usually occur in non-wetlands, but may occur in wetlands.

UPL (Upland Plants)—Almost never occur in wetlands.

Gary R. Sanford

APPENDIX 2

Growth habits and definitions are taken from:
https://plants.usda.gov/core/profile.

PLANTS Description	PLANTS Definition	Note
Forb/herb	Vascular plant without significant woody tissue above or at the ground. Forbs and herbs may be annual, biennial, or perennial but always lack significant thickening by secondary woody growth and have perennating buds borne at or below the ground surface. In PLANTS, graminoids are excluded but ferns, horsetails, lycopods, and whisk-ferns are included.	Applies to vascular plants only. Federal Geographic Data Committee (FGDC) definition includes graminoids, forbs, and ferns.
Graminoid	Grass or grass-like plant, including grasses (Poaceae), sedges (Cyperaceae), rushes (Juncaceae), arrow-grasses (Juncaginaceae), and quillworts (*Isoetes*).	Applies to vascular plants only. An herb in the FGDC classification.
Lichenous	Organism generally recognized as a single "plant" that consists of a fungus and an alga or cyanobacterium living in symbiotic association. Often attached to solid objects such as rocks or living or dead wood rather than soil.	Applies to lichens only, which are not true plants.
Nonvascular	Nonvascular, terrestrial green plant, including mosses, hornworts, and liverworts.	Applies to non-vascular plants only; in PLANTS system this is groups

PLANTS Description	PLANTS Definition	Note
	Always herbaceous, often attached to solid objects such as rocks or living or dead wood rather than soil.	HN (Hornworts), LV (Liverworts), and MS (Mosses).
Shrub	Perennial, multi-stemmed woody plant that is usually less than 4 to 5 meters (13 to 16 feet) in height. Shrubs typically have several stems arising from or near the ground, but may be taller than 5 meters or single-stemmed under certain environmental conditions.	Applies to vascular plants only.
Subshrub	Low-growing shrub usually under 0.5 m (1.5 feet) tall, never exceeding 1 meter (3 feet) tall at maturity.	Applies to vascular plants only. A dwarf-shrub in the FGDC classification.
Tree	Perennial, woody plant with a single stem (trunk), normally greater than 4 to 5 meters (13 to 16 feet) in height; under certain environmental conditions, some tree species may develop a multi-stemmed or short growth form (less than 4 meters or 13 feet in height).	Applies to vascular plants only.
Vine	Twining/climbing plant with relatively long stems, can be woody or herbaceous.	Applies to vascular plants only. FGDC classification considers woody vines to be shrubs and herbaceous vines to be herbs.

INFORMATION SOURCES

Fletcher, P. 1993. Soil Survey of Barnstable County, Massachusetts. Technical report of the U.S. Department of Agriculture, Soil Conservation Service.
Available:
https://www.nrcs.usda.gov/wps/portal/nrcs/detail/ma/soils/surveys/?cid=nrcs144p2_013984

Gucker, Corey L. 2007. Pinus rigida. In: Fire Effects Information System, [Online]. U.S. Department of Agriculture, Forest Service, Rocky Mountain Research Station, Fire Sciences Laboratory (Producer). 2012, November 24
Available:
https://www.feis-crs.org/feis/

Lichvar, R.W., D.L. Banks, W.N. Kirchner, and N.C. Melvin. 2016. The National Wetland Plant List: 2016 wetland ratings. Phytoneuron 2016-30: 1-17. Published 28 April 2016. ISSN 2153 733X.
Available:
http://wetland-plants.usace.army.mil/nwpl_static/v33/home/home.html

Lichvar, R. W., N. C. Melvin, M. L. Butterwick, & W. N. Kirchner. July 2012. National Wetland Plant List; Indicator Rating Definitions. U.S. Army Corps of Engineers, Engineer Research and Development Center, Cold Regions Research and Engineering Laboratory, Hanover, NH, and BONAP, Chapel Hill, NC. ERDC/CRREL TN-12-1.
Available:
https://www.fws.gov/wetlands/documents/National-Wetland-Plant-List-Indicator-Rating-Definitions.pdf

Little L. and P. W. Garrett 1990. Pinus rigida Mill. Pitch Pine. IN: R. M. Burns and B. H. Honkala, (tech. Coords.). Silvics of North America 1. Conifers; 2. Hardwoods. Publication: Agriculture Handbook 654, U.S. Dept. of Agriculture, Forest Service.
Available:
https://www.srs.fs.usda.gov/pubs/misc/ag_654/volume_1/pinus/rigida.htm

NRCS Plant Guide: RED MAPLE Acer rubrum L. USDA NRCS National Plant Data Center & the Biota of North America Program.
Available:
https://www.plants.usda.gov/plantguide/pdf/pg_acru.pdf

NRCS Plant Guide: Saltmeadow Cordgrass. Contributed by: USDA NRCS Rose Lake Plant Materials Center.
Available:
https://plants.usda.gov/plantguide/pdf/pg_sppa.pdf

NRCS Plant Guide: Smooth Cordgrass. Contributed By: USDA, NRCS, Louisiana State Office.
Available:
https://plants.usda.gov/plantguide/pdf/pg_spal.pdf

Stein, John, D. Binion, & R. Acciavatti. 2003. Field Guide to Native Oak Species of Eastern North America, USDA Forest Service, FHTET-2003-01.
Available:
https://www.fs.fed.us/foresthealth/technology/pdfs/fieldguide.pdf

Tirmenstein, D. A. 1991. Acer rubrum. In: Fire Effects Information System, [Online]. U.S. Department of Agriculture, Forest Service, Rocky Mountain Research Station, Fire Sciences Laboratory (Producer). 2012, February 11.
Available:
https://www.feis-crs.org/feis/

USGS. GEOLOGIC HISTORY OF CAPE COD, MASSACHUSETTS
Available:
https://pubs.usgs.gov/gip/capecod/index.html

Walkup, C. J. 1991. Spartina alterniflora. In: Fire Effects Information System, [Online]. U.S. Department of Agriculture, Forest Service, Rocky Mountain Research Station, Fire Sciences Laboratory (Producer).
Available:
https://www.feis-crs.org/feis/

Walkup, Crystal J. 1991. Spartina patens. In: Fire Effects Information System, [Online]. U.S. Department of Agriculture, Forest Service, Rocky Mountain Research Station, Fire Sciences Laboratory (Producer).
Available:
https://www.feis-crs.org/feis/

Walters, R. S. and Harry W. Yawney. 1990. Acer rubrum L. Red Maple IN: R. M. Burns and B. H. Honkala, (tech. Coords.). Silvics of North America 1. Conifers; 2. Hardwoods. Publication: Agriculture Handbook 654, U.S. Dept. of Agriculture, Forest Service.
Available:
https://www.srs.fs.usda.gov/pubs/misc/ag_654/volume_2/acer/rubrum.htm

Web Soil Survey. USDA Natural Resources Conservation Service – Soils
Available:
https://www.nrcs.usda.gov/wps/portal/nrcs/main/soils/survey/

ABOUT THE AUTHOR

Gary Sanford spent his youth on a ranch near Sebastopol, California, where agricultural products included eggs, apples, and cherries. After obtaining a Ph.D. in botany from the University of California, Davis campus, he moved to Massachusetts in the early 1970s, and has spent the last 45+ years in New England. Most of this time was spent working as an environmental consultant and botanist. The past few years have been devoted to non-fiction writing. He co-authored "The Ecology of Common Woody Plants of Cape Cod" and "Chester: A Buddy Forever". He also authored "It's Never To Late To Lose Some Weight".

(email - garysanford43@gmail.com)